Redamancy

a collection of love poems by

KAT SAVAGE

Redamancy

ISBN-13: 978-1537183466
ISBN-10: 153718346X

Also by Kat Savage

Mad Woman

Anchors & Vacancies

For Chris.

You make me feel
all warm and stuff
in my heart area.
And for that,
I love you.

In the Beginning, You Pray

We
  fell
    hopelessly
      into a love
I'm not sure either of us
truly understood.
All I could do
was hold on to you
as
  we
    tumbled
      through the pandemonium
of ripping our hearts from our bodies
and
handing them over to each other
as we both prayed like hell
that this time
it would be worth it.

Self-Inflicted

He is my favorite Beatles song
playing on repeat
while sipping coffee
on lazy Sunday mornings.

My lungs are playing
hide-and-seek
with the laugh lines
framing his eyes,

and I know,
I know I could've loved him
much sooner than now,

had I allowed myself.

Palms for Kissing

My lover bends to kiss the center
of my open palm
and it engulfs me,
as if he is kissing the most intimate
part of me,
the whole of who I am.

And I will use these tiny hands
to make sure he knows
they were always
meant for him.

All that I am
has always been
meant for him.

We All Want to Spin

You place a single kiss
on my collarbone.
And all the world shifts
on its axis.
And all the world dizzies me.

Suddenly I am a little girl
and I'm spinning in circles so fast
I will surely topple over
and fall into you
or
lift off and fly away.

The satisfaction is in
not knowing which one.

Rosetta Doesn't Have It

He is all the things
I haven't found words for yet,
but I want to keep trying.
He is moon rocks in my pockets
and a sky smudged purple
in the morning,
like maybe some kind of god
ran their thumb across
the sunrise.
Language, it has failed me.
There are no words for
what he makes me feel.
It didn't exist before now.

His Body Is a Journey That Has Journeyed to Here

I bet your body is magnificent.
I bet you don't even know it.

You said seventeen broken bones
and I heard,

> *I've carried some weight.*

You said two skin grafts and third degree burns
and I heard,

> *I've walked through fire and lived to tell*
> *you about it.*

You said twelve surgeries
and I heard,

> *I was pulled apart and stitched back*
> *together so I know what it means to be*
> *broken.*

You said three gunshot wounds
and I heard,

> *They tried to kill me but I couldn't let them*
> *do that because I had to get here.*
> *I had to make it to you.*

You told me you've been around the world and

seen some things
and I heard,

> My body made it all the way here to
> this moment so I could wrap my arms
> around you.

I bet your body is magnificent.
I bet you don't even know it.

I am Thief

Another nightmare takes hold of him.
Another 2am is stolen from us
as he lunges up
covered in a cold sweat,
grabs at the sheets,
and gasps for the breath
the monsters in his mind
took from him.

He doesn't know where he is just yet,
still hasn't come back to me.
I reach for his forearm,
touch him gently,
remind him.

I can see it in his eyes now.
He's back home but still afraid.
He folds into me,
wraps his arms around me,
buries his head as far into my chest
as my flesh will let him.

I place kisses on his forehead,
feel the thick beat of his heart calm.
I don't know where he is when
the nightmares of his yesterdays

take him.
I just hope I'm always here to pull him
back to this bed,
back to me.

I will fight his demons
every witching hour
until they are tired of hearing
my name.

Invisible Strings

He has this subtle way
of holding my hand
that makes me feel
like he is embracing
my entire body.
And that place
where his thumb traces
circles on my skin
has a direct line
to my heart.

Moments So Real

He is looking at me
and he is whispering
 "You are so beautiful"
into the
flushed red & fluttering flesh
above my heart.
He is so close
I can feel the heat
from his breath
roll across my skin
and something stills
in my chest.
This moment is so real
that I'm convinced
it's the first time
I've ever truly believed
those words
when spoken to me.

Saying Three Words

I catch the tip of my tongue
before it runs away from me
and says something I am afraid to.
Every moment before this one
has been leading me here.

I am standing in front of him,
and he is kissing me
between smiles.
I can feel a tremble
all the way to my soles.

And this moment,
this one here, now,
eyes fixed on him,
him staring back,
his arms around me,
mine tucked into his,
this is it.

I think even the sun knows,
because it has dipped behind
a bank of clouds
as if to bow its head.

I fell in love with him two dates ago
but I didn't let myself believe it
until now.
And it's all so terrifying
because I have never known
a peace like this.

Secret Moments

I catch you looking at me
and inquire.

"No," you say. "That moment is for me."

And I think I know what you mean
because when we're out to dinner
and I'm watching your face animate
a story you're telling me,
sometimes my ears muffle
what you're saying and I am
taking in every detail of your face,
every flick of your wrist,
every shrug of your shoulder.
I am breathing you in
one mannerism at a time.

And I get lost there
for longer than I intend.

So if you should find yourself
lost in your admiration for me,
take all the time you need.
I'll be here when you return.
And there is no need to share
because I have moments of my own.

Hardwood Oceans Between Lovers

We built this floor
from the driftwood
we found on the beach
that day we fell in love.
Now it holds up the four-poster
you take me in most nights.

On Sunday mornings,
it's cold on my feet
and forces me back
under an ocean of blankets
where you wait for me.

On this particular morning,
you pulled me into you while
James Bay played in the background
and we danced over
salt-licked and sea foam
hardwood waters.

And I know,
I know there will never be
anything more than
these few inches between us.

A Heart Like Flypaper

My heart,
it lies here,
all sugar cane and honey,
but I can't tell anyone that.

They want the decay.

Not him.
He drinks me in.
All the nectar,
all the goodness.

He loves my love poems
and my laugh
and my happiness
and so I will
give him all of my
sticky sweet mess
and watch him lick it
from his fingertips.

Cliché Love Poem

You are the night sky
and I lie here with you,
tracing over all the
starlit freckles
on your porcelain skin.

I am an astronomer
mapping constellations
and naming them
for all the reasons
I love you.

It's Not What You Think

The heel of my foot
is resting gently against
your clavicle.
(I know what you're all thinking
but you're wrong.)
You are caressing lotion
on to my thighs and studying
the ink on them,
while I study your face
and wonder what you are wondering.
There is nothing sexual or
provocative about the way
your hands are moving.
There is only a tender
intimacy.
There is only this.
You love me.
And I feel it.

Just After the Parthenon

We are wrapped up in Nashville,
wrapped up in this hotel room,
wrapped up in these linens,
wrapped up in each other.
And the room is spinning
but you say you like that.
And I am high on that feeling
I get in the back of my knees
when you lift my legs into the air.
Everything is
white hot
dirty crazy
intense new
passion sex
lust.
And everything is
sky blue
melty comfortable
intimate
love.

A Comment I left on His Instagram Photo of the Parthenon in Nashville, TN

You are on an airplane on your way back to this place and I am lying here in bed and I have this large purple elephant stuffed under my arm and I try to make it a whole person when I'm not in bed with you but I can never manage to stretch it far enough. I think I overwatered our love cactus and by love cactus I mean the cactus you gave me because you said it would be impossible to kill. But don't worry, I Googled how to save it and with any luck I will save it. There are three orange flavored energy drinks in my refrigerator and I blame you but I wouldn't have it any other way. The book I ordered for you came in the mail today and I stared down at the address label wondering what it would look like with both our names on it. There's a rubber ducky in the bottom of my purse from that game place and I'm leaving it there just for you. I will be in Nashville again in two months and it will not be the same Nashville we shared. I was sad it rained on your one day in Hawaii but then I thought, *We will just have to go back when it isn't.* I wrote myself a note to get a passport application from the post office tomorrow so we can go to all

the places you've been and the ones on our list,
too. These, and so many more, are the tiny little
things I see and feel and think between each
breath. And then my lungs fill. And I know I am in
love with you. You are splashed across my life so
delicately, it's as if you've always been here.

We Gave Something Up

The excitement.
The energy.
The newness.
There is a moment
when it all shifts.
These things don't go far
but they do go away.
It makes room for other things.
Like trust,
and comfort,
and a deeper affection.
They bloom in your body
in all the places
you had forgotten
were in need of them.
And that's when you know
nothing will ever
be the same
again.

He Makes Me Feel Everything

Sometimes
there is no grand poem
to be written,
no long drawn out
explanation
for the *whys* or *hows*.
Sometimes everything
you need to say
can be wrapped up
in a single sentence
and there's no need
to complicate it,
no need to pollute it
with subpar words.
He makes me feel
            e v e r y t h i n g
after too long of nothing.
and that is enough.
That is
            e v e r y t h i n g.

How We Lie

Your head is resting gingerly
on my inner thigh and you are
looking up at me and smiling.

This is where you've come
to rest after tasting me
and this is how we will lie
and talk
and laugh.

You—
between my parted legs.
Me—
cradling you in such a way
it is both
the most arousing thing I've ever felt
and the most comfortable.

This is how we lie—
together.

Revelations in Your Camaro

I can smell your cologne
on the front of my blouse
and there is a tingling
in my wrists where you kissed them.

It was senior year all over again
and you were
all the butterflies of my first boyfriend
but none of the sadness.

We made out in your car
like a couple of kids
that had nowhere to be
and you cranked the music up loud
so your whole car shook
just to admit to me that
as a 31-year-old man,
you spend money on things you shouldn't.
But it makes you happy
and so I don't really think
it's all that silly.
We all need to feel the music
in our throats sometimes.

And maybe I'm not yet brave enough
to sing along but you'll get it out of me

one of these days.
My song is buried down
in my neglected ribcage
with all the things
people have forgotten to ask about.
And you don't understand those people.
But you'll gladly ask the questions.
And I like that.

Goodnight Text

My dear,
two days until I touch you
and two days has never
felt more like forever
than it does now.
My skin aches for your skin
and only the softness of your lips
will soothe my rigid bones.

To Give and Receive

You thanked me
for taking care of you
and I looked at you funny
because in that moment
I realized
no lover has ever thanked me
for taking care of them.
And no lover has ever
taken care of you.
If I've ever been
both happy and sad
at the same time,
I can't think of
a better instance than this.
I'm sad neither of us
ever had what we deserved
but I'm happy we do now.
I will spend
the rest of my time with you
showing you
what it feels like
to be truly loved.

I'm Yours

I just wanted to say it out loud
one time
in case my actions failed me,
in case there was any doubt
in your mind or in your heart,
in case you thought otherwise
for even a split second,
in case you've become used to
too many lies and not enough
truths,
in case I can't say it tomorrow,
in case there is a meteor
while we're sleeping
or a zombie apocalypse next week,
in case we get into an argument
and both forget for a moment,
in case I've failed to tell you before now,

I'm yours.

Learning What We Means

He turned my /into *we*
over and over again
until I believed it,
and
I let myself feel
everything I had
discarded over the years.
I'm not alone anymore.
And there's no need to
shoulder it all myself
when he knows the weight
of my life
and considers it
a privilege to help carry it.

And So He Fights On

He hates my past.
Rather,
the pain in it
that forced me to build walls,
to stay guarded.

He can't erase it.
He can't undo it.
He knows that.

But every day he fights
to give me reasons
to believe that everything
before now wasn't worthy
of me,
that I am too good
to have ever been given
all that sorrow.

And I'm starting to believe him.

He Is Not Made of Metaphors

You will find no lilac
laced in my lover's mouth.
He tastes like
spearmint toothpaste
and Marlboro Menthols
and on occasion a round of
Jameson with a splash of water.

There are no stars or diamonds
sparkling in his eyes.
But they are so crystalline blue
I can see my reflection in them
and I understand what people mean
when they say they can see their future
in another's.

His hands are not magic
but I find myself tracing over
the tiny scars on his knuckles
and returning his kisses in kind.

My lover isn't made of metaphors.
He is real and I feel him
just as I feel my own heart
beating in my chest
even when he isn't here.

Drunk Poem (Not to Be Confused With Drunk Text)

It's Friday night
and I'm drinking wine
and it's hot in here
and by in here I mean
inside this vessel
I call my body.
But this warmth
does not compare
to your warmth,
and I'd much rather
have you inside me
than the wine.

Over and Over Again

I am twenty minutes late
for work just so I can sit in my car
and take the perfect photo of my sunrise
to send him.
Because he needs to see what I see,
and it's no longer my sunrise,
it's ours.

I get to fall in love with him every day
while some won't even get to do it once.
So I consider myself lucky.
Or cursed.
Or both.

But ask me what my favorite
time of the day is and I'll say it
again and again—
just a little after seven in the morning
when I'm late for work and the sky is orange
and I'm trading secrets like
baseball cards
and falling in love
for the third time this week.

A Short Story About That Time We Cooked Dinner

It's utter chaos in my kitchen. Two adults and three children. He is chopping things, surrounded by tiny helpful hands, and I am trying to keep my son out of the dish water in the sink and away from the stove.

The girls are touching everything with their little hands and his patience is thicker than mine. We carry things over to the stove and my son cuts his finger while trying to chop an onion and it's more chaos. My son is crying and I am rushing around for a bandage and I can't find any ointment and I feel despair wash over me as I settle into feeling like the worst mother ever.

He goes to the freezer and places an ice cube on my son's finger. And my son isn't crying anymore. Now the food on the stove needs to be stirred and the girls want to do the dishes and everyone is everywhere and I think I might crack.

We get a silent moment and I tell him I'm sorry. Sorry for all of it. Sorry for the chaos, sorry for all the excitement, all the kids. Sorry, for my life.

Because I've become accustomed to needing to apologize for it.

He turns to me, and he says,
"How long is it going to take?"

I look over at the food.
"I'm not sure," I say.

He says, "No. How long is it going to take for me to prove to you that I'm here and I'm not going anywhere and there is nothing for you to be sorry for?"

Sometimes the question is the answer.

Small but Significant

You sit across from me in the restaurant
and talk about all your goals and what you
hope to accomplish for the year.

My breath catches for a moment
because you're not saying my name
and I wonder if you've left me out
on purpose.

Then your hand brushes over mine
on the table and you say,
"Of course, you'll be there too,
won't you?"

And all the world feels right again
because I am here across from you
and I am in your future, too.

American Sign Language

You are signing the alphabet to me.
Practicing.
I am signing it back to you just for fun.
I study the way your fingers move
as they form my favorite letters.
B. K. R. Y.
I like the placement for these.
I like that your mouth moves for each,
making the shape but not the sound.

You sign, "I love you."

I know, baby. I know.
My heart knows your heart
like your hands know the alphabet.

They Took It for Granted

I lather shampoo into your shoulder-length hair,
starting at the temples and working my way
back through each strand.
I feel your body slump and lean into me
as you relax into now.
Your mouth releases an audible sigh
and I watch your eyes flutter
beneath your lids
as the water cascades over
your freckled skin.

I cannot figure out why no one has ever
let you know exactly how beautiful you are.

Sleepless Nights

On nights we are apart,
I lie in my nearly empty bed
and pretend I will be able to sleep.

I spend the next two hours
tossing and turning.
I arrange my pillows in a crescent shape
and throw my leg over them.
These pillows are not you
and I can't remember why I thought
they would do a sufficient job
of filling in for you.

I am doing the calendar math in my head,
breaking down the days to hours,
the hours to minutes,
the minutes to moments,
and thinking about how many more
sleepless moments there are
between the two of us.

There are too many.
There are always too many.
And there will be too many
until there are none.

I Stumble on This Newness

He tucks my hair behind my ear,
lips brushing against the lobe.

"I am so into you,"
he says, voice low and sincere.
He kisses the dip in my jaw,
pulls me closer by the loops
of my jeans.

I stumble,
on my own feet,
on the lump in my throat,
on his words.

But I never fall.
He is always there,
always right next to me,
ready to pull me back up.

It's new.
And scary.
And wonderful.

At Home Under His Touch

His movements were slow.
Deliberate.
Intoxicating.
He sought to watch me come
u
n
d
o
n
e
in his bed
beneath his touch.
I fell away.
No decisions to make,
blurry edges,
the taste of wine
between our lips.
I gave in to the little voice inside me—
I rode the tide,
waves crashing over me
again and again.

He made my skin less foreign.
I was finally familiar with myself.

Redamancy

I sit silently
wrapped up in the warmth
of a love that travels down my throat
like warm coffee.
It starts in the center of me
and crashes outward in waves
over and over again.

This is what all of us ache for,
hope for, wish on stars for.
This is what all the coins in every
fountain have whispered into them.

Give me redamancy.
      Give me redamancy.
            Give me redamancy.
            Give me you.
      Give me you.
Give me you.
Give me us.
      Give me us.
            Give me us.

And that's really what all of this
has been about.
Us.

About the Author

Kat Savage is a single mom of two, works full-time, and manages to jot a few words down here and there in her spare time. She has a degree in graphic design and takes advantage of it to design all her own books as well as others' on a freelance basis. This year, she fell in love and she wanted you to know.

Kat Savage is also very active on social media and wants you to semi-stalk her.

Follow her on Instagram:
@kat.savage

Like her on Facebook:
Facebook.com/katsavagepoetry

Tweet her on Twitter:
@thekatsavage

Connect with her (you can shop here too!):
www.thekatsavage.com

Made in the USA
Lexington, KY
08 January 2017